Matador
9 Priory Business Park,
Wistow Road,
Kibworth Beauchamp
Leicester LE8 0RX UK
Tel: (+44) 116 279 2299
Fax: (+44) 116 279 2277
Email: books@troubador.co.uk
Web: www.troubador.co.uk/matador

Published in South Africa by Sunbird Publishers (Pty) Ltd
PO box 6836, Roggebaai, 8012, Cape Town, South Africa
www.sunbirdpublishers.co.za
Registration number: 1984/003543/07

Photograph of the author by Matthias Braune

ISBN 978-1848767-690

British Library Cataloguing in Publication Data.
A catalogue record for this book is available from the British Library.

Book design by Terry Compton, Troubador Publishing Ltd, Leicester, UK

Matador is an imprint of Troubador Publishing Ltd

Dedicated to my parents who first introduced me to the natural world, the many people who give their lives to the conservation of this beautiful region, and of course to the animals themselves.

The Realm of the Desert Elephant

Kaokoland and Damaraland

Photography and text by Chris Wildblood

Contents

1. Introduction   xii

2. Kaokoland and Damaraland   1
    (Kunene Region)

3. The Wildlife   20

4. The Elephants   52

5. The Himba   78

6. The Skeleton Coast   90

6. Behind the Camera   114

7. Acknowledgements   122

Namibia and its Position in Africa

ANGOLA

ZAMBIA

Kunene

Ruacana

KAOKOLAND

Kavango

Opuwo

Ondangwa

Rundu

Caprivi Game Park

Kongola

Katima Mulilo

Andara

Skeleton Coast Park

Etosha National Park

Mudumu National Park

Warmquelle

Etosha Pan

Khaudum Game Park

DAMARALAND

Okaukuejo

Tsumeb

Kamanjab

Otavi

Grootfontein

Tsumkwe

Skeleton Coast

Torran Bay

Outjo

Waterberg Plateau Park

Khorixas

Otjiwarongo

Brandberg
△
2573m

Kalkfeld

NAMIBIA

Omaruro

Usakos

Okahandja

NORTH

0   200 km
0   100 miles

Henties Bay

Khomas Hochland

WINDHOEK

Gobabis

BOTSWANA

Swakopmund

Walvis Bay

Namib Desert

Rehoboth

ATLANTIC OCEAN

Namib-Naukluft Park

Kalkrand

Aranos

Maltahöhe

Mariental

Fish

Kalahari Desert

Lüderitz

Bethanie

Keetmanshoop

Seeheim

Aroab

Huib-Hoch Plateau

Grünau

Groot Karasberge

Ai-Ais/Richtersveld Transfrontier Park

Karasburg

Orange

SOUTH AFRICA

DEMEMOCRATIC REPUBLIC OF THE CONGO

TANZANIA

ANGOLA

ZAMBIA

MALAWI

Kaokoland Damaraland

ZIMBABWE

MOZAMBIQUE

MADAGASCAR

NAMIBIA

BOTSWANA

SWAZILAND

ATLANTIC OCEAN

SOUTH AFRICA

LESOTHO

INDIAN OCEAN

Alison Davis/Mapping Company

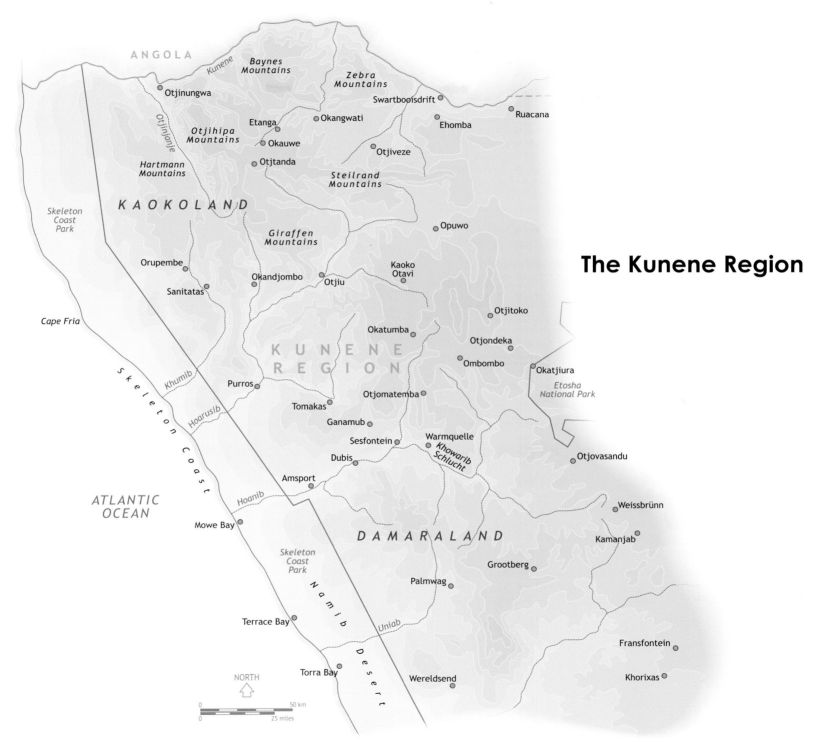

The Kunene Region

ANGOLA

Kunene

Baynes Mountains

Zebra Mountains

Otjinungwa

Swartbooisdrift

Okangwati

Otjinjanje

Etanga

Ehomba

Ruacana

Otjihipa Mountains

Okauwe

Otjiveze

Hartmann Mountains

Otjtanda

Steilrand Mountains

Skeleton Coast Park

KAOKOLAND

Giraffen Mountains

Opuwo

Orupembe

Kaoko Otavi

Okandjombo

Otjiu

Cape Fria

Sanitatas

Otjitoko

KUNENE REGION

Okatumba

Otjondeka

Ombombo

Okatjiura

Purros

Etosha National Park

Otjomatemba

Tomakas

Ganamub

Skeleton Coast

Khumib

Hoarusib

Sesfontein

Warmquelle

Khowarib Schlucht

Otjovasandu

Dubis

Amsport

Hoanib

ATLANTIC OCEAN

Mowe Bay

Weissbrünn

DAMARALAND

Kamanjab

Skeleton Coast Park

Grootberg

Palmwag

Terrace Bay

Namib Desert

Uniab

Fransfontein

Torra Bay

Wereldsend

Khorixas

NORTH

0 — 50 km
0 — 25 miles

Alison Davis/Mapping Company

Introduction

Having been lucky enough to have travelled to many parts of the world through my work as a photographer (and loved many parts of it), it was my first visit to Kaokoland and Damaraland that sealed my thoughts about where I wanted to work for the next few years.

The pristine scenery is stunning, and the wildlife is wonderful, having lived there for eons without too much intervention from man.

This book is not meant to be a guide to the region (you wont find any roads on the maps), purely a record of what I found and saw on my adventures. I can only hope that I have managed to do it justice.

It does need to be gently respected and cared for though, and hopefully not exploited, otherwise we will loose yet another part of our beautiful planet.

Chris Wildblood.
2012

Foreword

by Steve Braine

Louise, the boys and I were privileged to spend 21 years at Hobatere Lodge in Northwestern Namibia. During this time we met many interesting folk – some scientists, artists, moviemakers, and photographers. This is how we met Chris, while on his travels in Namibia. He became a friend and an inspiration to all amateur photographers visiting the lodge, sharing his enthusiasm and passion for photography with everybody. Chris would then "disappear" into the vastness of Damaraland and Kaokoland and re-appear after several weeks, weather beaten, exhausted and with a huge grin on his dust covered face, in anticipation to show his incredible photos.

Chris manages to capture the beauty and uniqueness of the vast open spaces and unspoiled terrain as well as the diverse wildlife of Damaraland and Kaokoland. That he cares about the animals and the environment is clearly depicted in his work. With this book, Chris hopes to inspire readers and photographers alike, but at the same time have everybody that browse through it, ultimately respect this pristine wildlife and untouched wilderness.

The **Kunene Region**

A vast and magical land

Sculptured by tectonics, eroded by ice, wind, water and heat for hundreds of millions of years.

Timeless...

The falls at Ruacana on the Kunene River

N amibia is a large country with an area of 825,418sq km making it over twice the size of Germany and three and a half times the size of the United Kingdom. The name Namibia is derived from the Namib Desert, considered to be the oldest desert in the world, and the name 'Namib' comes from an ancient word meaning 'barrier'. Tucked up in the north west corner of the country, bordered by the Kunene river in the north and the Skeleton Coast lining the South Atlantic Ocean to the west lies the Kunene Region, formally known as Kaokoland and Damaraland.

For those that have been luckily enough to have visited the region, these names conjure up images of harsh unforgiving mountains, their rocks torn apart by the savage heat, beautiful lush green landscapes after the rains, the magnificent Kunene river that flows perennially in the north, the wonderful unique wildlife and the home of the Himba.

The Kunene river at dawn

'Damaraland' is the southern of the two regions and is the relatively 'gentler' one of the two. It has a reasonable infrastructure of roads, electricity, water supplies to towns and villages, cell-phone coverage is marching forever onwards, old gravel roads are being replaced by new tarmac 'highways' and good shops, where supplies can be found, in most of the larger communities. The scenery is beautiful, from the rocky plains with their special black rhino of the Palmwag area to the west, the table-top mountains that give Etendecka camp it's name and the lands to the west of Etosha that is Hobatere with it's rich diversity of wildlife.

To the north of 'Damaraland' lies 'Kaokoland'. Officially this starts at the Hoanib river which dissects the country east to west, trying to reach the South Atlantic when in flood, but failing, due to the relentless march of the dunes of the Skeleton Coast.

You don't really notice the transition travelling between the two but once there, you know you are somewhere special.

Here you are on your own.

'Kaokoland' is possibly the most unspoilt, untouched wilderness of Sub-Saharan Africa. Even the Serengeti has been shaped by mankind over thousands of years.

'The Hoanib, the 'border' between Damaraland and Kaokoland'

It is not a National Park, but due to it's harsh conditions, lack of infrastructure and inaccessibility, it doesn't need to be (yet). However, it does need to be looked after and not over exploited. If the idea of damming the Kunene for hydro electricity (whether good or bad) ever comes to fruition, then it's remoteness will be lost forever. Here the animals live as they have since time immemorial, they follow the rains, springs and the foliage of the ephemeral riverbeds that sustain them, occasionally coming into conflict with humans, but usually coming to some kind of an amicable acceptance or understanding. The Himba people have learnt to live here as well, after moving back from Angola after the war, and co-exist with the wildlife, although the elephants tend to irritate them when they eat all their crops.

Top: The Marrienflus Valley
Bottom: Kaokoland showing its harsher side

Kaokoland is unforgettable and totally unique. Whether you are in the Hartsmann valley or the Marienfluss for the scenery, on the Kunene river looking for the elusive cinderella waxbills or relaxing at Epupa falls, exploring the dry riverbeds from Purros searching for the elephants or desert lions, it will not disappoint.

The land has been formed over millennia. Colossal tectonic and volcanic forces millions of years ago formed a land that makes any geologist think they have gone to heaven.

★★★

Many more millions of years of erosion by the relentless heat of the sun, the desert winds sand-blasting everything in their path, even glaciation periods (before plate-tectonics did their thing), and the rivers scouring out their valleys, fertilising the floodplains and bringing new life each year to the riparian woodlands that follow the river courses on their way to try to find the sea.

Left: The Kunene River looking East at dawn.
Next Page: The spectacular Kohowarib Schlucht

For most of the year the riverbeds look dry, but underneath there is always water, seeping slowly downhill and westwards towards the ocean. Occasionally the water meets an impervious layer of rock that forces it to the surface forming a sparkling linear oasis that may flow for several kilometers (an example of which can be found at the western end of the Khowarib Schlucht), or possibly a brackish oasis or maybe only just enough to dampen the sand. Elephants can sense this water under the surface (which us humans would think was bone-dry desert sand) and dig large 'xoras' (holes) to get to the sweet naturally filtered water. These Xoras then subsequently help the other animals in the area.

Rainfall generally comes from the east, usually in two wet seasons. The first rains, known as the 'Little Rains' arrive around October, but have a tendency to do not a lot more than to settle the dust. The second rains arrive any time from January onwards and this is the life-blood of the region. As the summer heat builds up, huge thunder clouds form over the central highlands and unleash their anger on the earth as they march westwards across the country. To see an African thunderstorm in this vast beautiful landscape with it's deafening thunder, wall to wall lightening and torrents of water is to witness one of our planet's amazing natural wonders.

The rainfall usually falls towards the eastern side of the region, with less falling the further west you travel due to the drop in altitude, the clouds running out of steam, and the influence of the cold Benguella current sweeping up the coast from Antarctica.

Dawn over the 'Table Top' or 'Etendeka' mountains.

Gradually as the ground gets more and more saturated over the following weeks, the rivers begin to flow, as opposed to the water simply sinking into the ground. In some years when rainfall is low the rivers may run for short periods and may never reach the sea, but other years (as in 2011) they form raging torrents that carry away everything in their path and reach the sea, turning it brown with silt and debris. We have yet to see what effect climate change will have on these cycles, but over the past few years flooding has become more commonplace. Even so, sometimes the rains fail, at times for a number of consecutive years. When this happens the results are devastating for both humans and wildlife.

When they do flow however, these ephemeral rivers form the basis for the riparian woodlands that follow their courses, occasionally interspersed with linear wetlands that can even support reeds and sedges, and consequently providing the vegetation needed to support the region's diverse range of wildlife.

The Kunene River looking from North to South, with Namibia in the background and Angoala in the foreground

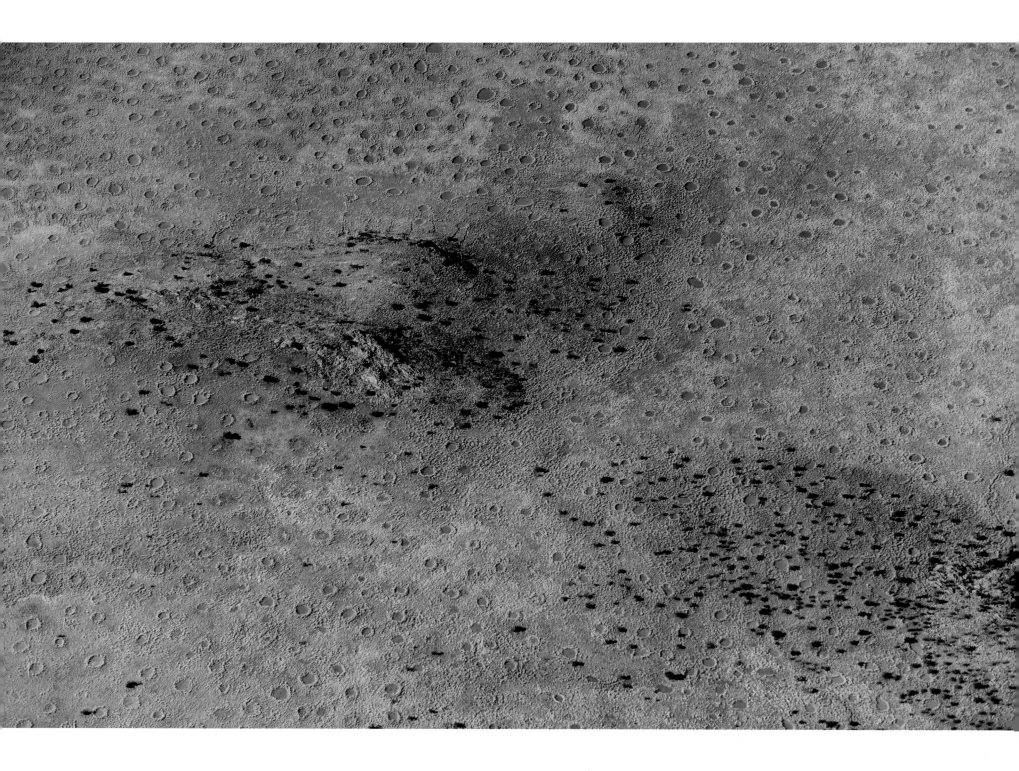

Fairy Circles

Now these are fun.

Fairy Circles are circular-ish patches of un-vegetated sandy ground, usually 3 to 10 meters across and are found in a broken stretch from the Orange river in the south, through the Namib Desert and on through Damaraland and Kaokoland, across the Kunene river and into Southern Angola

Around the edges, the grasses are taller, possibly due to extra moisture and minerals unused in the soil but probably due to grazing animals not wanting to eat that close to them for some reason that only they know. The same can also be seen at the edges of vehicle tracks throughout the areas where they are found.

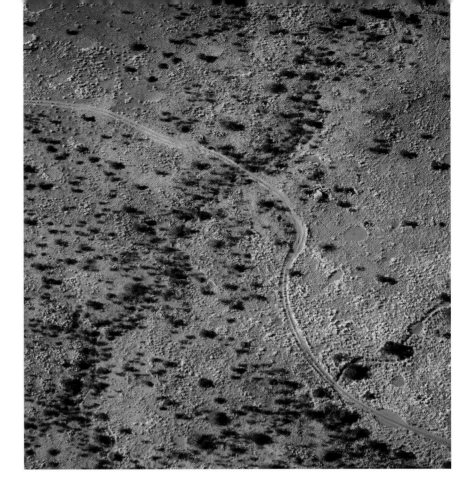

Countless 'scientists' have investigated the reasons for their formation and have come up with various explanations for their formation and existence, ranging from termites and noxious gasses seeping from underground, to poisonous plants (euphorbia) having grown there in the past or possibly even meteor showers.

Nobody has yet come up with a definitive theory and probably never will. Personally I prefer the 'aliens' theory....

A bit more Damaraland and Kaokoland 'Magic' to add to what is plentiful already.

16

Welwitchia Mirabillis

The 1000 year old living fossil

The Welwitschia grows from a short, thick, woody stem but with only two leaves, that continuously grow from their base, and a long, thick taproot .

After germination, the cotyledons grow up to 35mm in length, and are followed shortly afterward by the appearance of two permanent leaves. These leaves are produced on opposite sides of the cotyledons, and continue to grow throughout the entire life of the plant.

Eventually, they can grow to a length of 2 to 4 m and generally become split into several sections due to the actions of the wind, and inquisitive animals, thus disguising their origin from only two leaves. The species is dioecious, with separate male and female plants.

Fertilization, the transfer of the pollen from the male to the female strobili, is usually carried out by insects that are attracted by nectar produced on both male and female strobili, although wind may play a part.

17

Animals such as the oryx, rhino and springbok sometimes feed or nibble at them, but wind, sun and drought probably help more to their dessicrated appearance.

It is thought that they can live to between 1000 and 2000 years and they are only found in the north western area of Namibia and southern Angola, as although they have a deep tap-root, they are still able to make some use of the morning fogs that roll inland from the South Atlantic.

The **Wildlife**

The region, although classified as desert, semi-desert or arid, sustains a large amount of wildlife that has adapted to it's unforgiving climate.

Mother and baby giraffe in the Hoanib

Wildlife is dependent on the same limited resources of food and water as humans and livestock.

Elephants and rhinos, giraffe and lions, are amongst some of the many reasons visitors come to the area, along with many species of birds (many endemic), tranquility, and wonderful scenery.

The wildlife has fluctuated widely over the past few decades. In the 1960's the elephant population of Kaokoland and northern Damaraland was estimated to be between 1500-3000 and giraffe and black rhinos were reported to be numerous.

In the 1970's and 80's Damaraland and Kaokoland was subjected to unrestricted hunting by the military (during the bush war), professional hunters and poachers that decimated the wildlife populations to a fraction of their previous levels. This impact, together with a severe drought over several years, lead to the wildlife population decreasing even more.

Recently though they have been making an admirable comeback, mainly due to anti-poaching efforts and realization by the local people and the government, both regional and national, that the income generated by tourism is worth more in the long run than a short term gain.

Top: Giraffe on the gravel plains between the Hoanib and the Hourasib
Above: Klipspringer at Hobatere
Right: Hammercop in the Hourasib
Far right (top): Meerkats
Far right (bottom): A chameleon in one of it's many guises

Traveling through the region isn't like visiting a National park, for instance Kruger or Etosha where you have animals on tap, and when all you need to do is to draw up a list in the morning, of what you want to see, employ a guide with a radio, and hay presto by the end of the day you have most if not all of them ticked off.

No, here you are really on your own (or with a guide) and things take time. Depending on what you want to see it is best to do your research first, whether you want to watch cinderella waxbills by the Kunene, elephants in the riverbeds or the most amazing scenery that makes Tolkien's 'Lord of the Rings' look dull, it can all take time.

Life is pretty tough here, but all the animals, whether giraffe, elephant, leopard, springbok, vulture, scorpion or moths, have adapted to live here, and where they are without too much human intervention and conflict, they thrive.

They understand the seasons and take advantage of everything each one has to offer, whether through natural instinct or by watching and learning from their peers and making their own mistakes along the way.

Here you won't see herds of 150 elephants at a waterhole and it might even take you days to find your first one, nor will you see a leopard in every tree. But when you do, seeing it, in it's unchanged natural habitat, since time immemorial, you will never forget the experience.

Top right: A masked weaver finishing off his nest.
Bottom right: A cute but very irritating vervet monkey on the banks of the Kunene.
Opposit page: Giraffe and an oryx by the Hoanib

Left: *Two male giraffes testing their strength*
Above: *A female warthog having her daily bath*

Above: Oryx on the floor of the Marrenflus Valley
Opposite: Mountain Zebra enjoying the dust

Predators

Large carnivore populations in Namibia (outside protected areas) have decreased substantially in the past fifty years but some are slowly making a comeback.

This has been attributed largely to increased conflict with human development, resulting in contraction of the ranges of most species to their confinement to marginal habitats or within protected areas. Poaching and trophy hunting has also taken its fair share. However even protected areas do not offer full protection and large carnivore species often cause livestock losses along the borders and are persecuted.

Above: A spotted hyena returning home at dawn
Right: A sub-adult male lion on a recent kill

Large carnivores (and often elephants) form the spearhead of conflict between the ever increasing human population and their joint natural resources, Lions and leopards form the biggest problems as they are large enough to take down cattle, donkeys and goats (and sometimes humans) with ease. These prey have little or no instinct left to know how avoid a predator, so provide easy pickings.

In protection of their livestock, farmers often shoot, trap, or poison them. These local communities have to bear the costs of living with predators, but do not share equally in the benefits from tourism, and they receive little assistance in managing conflicts . Smaller, more timid predators like cheetah, caracal, bat-eared foxes and jackals do not tend to cause so much of a problem as they usually avoid humans where possible.

However, much work is being done by various NGOs and governmental departments to try and reverse the trends of the past, and in many instances to great effect.

Left: A black-backed jackal and vultures clean up after the lions have had their fill

In this region, probably the main contributor helping these animals is Dr P Stander of the Desert Lion Conservation Project and with his help the population of lions has been gradually increasing over a number of years, although trophy hunting is taking its toll.

There is still much to be done though, but people are beginning to realise just how important a healthy predator population is to the area, not only for tourism but also for nature to take its natural course and for the weak to be weeded out and the strongest and healthiest to survive.

www.desertlion.info

Left: A rather cute, young, male leopard
Above: A crocodile gets his lunch
Top right: A cheetah surveying his surroundings
Bottom right: A beautiful black-maned lion in his prime
Far right: Inquisitive bat-eared fox cubs

Left: Three cheetahs looking for a meal
Right: Mother and young male having a tender moment

Left: Spotted Hyena with his choice of the best bits
Above: Lesser-Spotted Gennet
Top Right: This is Mine!
Bottom Right: Leopard cub

The Black Rhino

(Diceros bicornis bicornis)

Namibia's desert-adapted black rhino *(Diceros bicornis bicornis)* that lives in the Damaraland region represent the only rhino worldwide that have survived on communal land with no formal conservation status. They are also the largest free-ranging black rhino population in the world.

Due to the scarcity of food resources in the arid Namib, these rhino are known to cover some 2,500 km^2 in search of food and water. They have very large home ranges, measuring 500 - 600 km^2. The dryness of the climate gives the skin of the rhino a smooth, glossy appearance. The footprints (spoor) are larger than other black rhino subspecies. These rhino have no lesions or visible parasites. Their mountaineering abilities are remarkable, they can climb high onto mountain ledges out of the heat of the valley, to catch the cool wind from the Atlantic or forage for succulents.

That these rhino can survive in areas with less than 100mm mean annual rainfall is amazing. Normally rhino drink every night, yet in the this arid region, because they must move great distances in search of food, they may drink only every third or even fourth day. Yet Damaraland's black rhinos remain heavily dependant upon undisturbed access to permanent water sources. Black rhino in the region, like other black rhino populations across Africa, tend to avoid areas utilized by humans and their livestock.

The rhino feed on an estimated 74 plant species of the 103 species that are available during the driest period of any year. Among the plants taken are several which contain very high levels of soluble tannins, which are usually regarded as a chemical defense against animal predation. The rhino feed extensively on Euphorbia virosa and damarana bushes. This plant is highly poisonous to humans and can cause blindness if the milk enters the eye. It is thought that the rhino evolved alongside the plant over millenia and so developed their tolerance.

The rhino also feed occasionally on Welwitschia mirabilis plants but normally just chew on the

leaves and extract the juices, before discarding the remaining fibrous portion.

The rhino show a distinct preference for certain other plants as well, and will return to preferred food plants to browse new growth. Fortunately such plants recover quickly after rain and put out new shoots. The rhino also feed on Welwitschia mirabilis plants but normally just chew on the leaves and extract the juices, before discarding the remaining fibrous portion.

Black rhino calves spend a minimum of two to two-and-a-half years with the cow in a specific part of her home range, before being weaned. The calf becomes well orientated, learning the whereabouts of water, mountain succulents and other food sources. The cow weans the calf and then moves out of the area to another part of her home range to give birth to her new calf. The weaned calf may join up periodically with the cow and new calf. These visits are not prolonged and the sub-adult rhino returns to the area that is familiar.

Adult rhino kick their dung and spray urine as a communication system while moving about their ranges, spreading their scent around and making dung middens along pathways near water holes.

Above: The Palmwag rhino country
Right: A bull rhino

Desert rhino have sometimes been observed in groups but are usually solitary except for cow/calf combinations. There is seldom fighting between bulls, but occasionally very aggressive bulls have been known to kill another bull. Cows have been observed to see off other cows with calves in overlapping home ranges.

Namibia's desert-adapted black rhino add a dimension of grandeur to the stunning scenery of the areas they inhabit. If conserved and utilized sensibly, these scenic areas and their wildlife will be preserved for generations to come.

The desert-adapted black rhino population is currently one of very few populations in Africa that is steadily increasing. This positive growth can only be assured while the current vigilant, monitoring and anti-poaching effort is maintained, mainly overseen and managed by Save the Rhino (or SRT) under the watchful eye of Rudy Loutit and others based at Palmwag.

www.savetherhinotrust.org

The Birdlife

Written and photographed by Steve and Dayne Braine.

Besides the large numbers of desert adapted fauna and flora within the Namib desert, this vast area of sand dunes, gravel plains, rocky outcrops and rugged mountains also harbour some unique avifauna (or birdlife). Several Namibian species have evolved in unique ways to exist in this harsh environment and, many do not need to drink, but get all their moisture requirements through the food that they feed on, such as 'juicy' stone hoppers, geckos and lizards. A few worth mentioning would be the Rüppell's Korhaan and Benguella Long-billed Lark and Tractrac Chat.

One of the more amazing adaptations is the water carrying capability of the Namaqua Sandgrouse (a species that needs to drink daily), whereby these birds collect water between their breast feathers and may fly up to 40 kilometres from a water source to give their chicks this life supporting resource from the adults feathers!

Right: Pearl-spotted Owlet
Far Right: Augur Buzzard

The only true endemic, the Dune Lark has also adapted to living in the vast sand sea of the Namib and gets its moisture from the insects on which it feeds.

On the eastern verges of the arid desert, where the open desert plains reach the escarpment, pushed up millions of years ago by dynamic tectonic plate movements, we begin to encounter stunted vegetation. Dry river beds (linear oasis) leading to the Atlantic Ocean are also found bisecting the Namib desert from east to west. It is in these river beds that many other species such as the Madagascar (Olive) Bee-eater, Pearl-spotted Owlet, African Scops Owl (the smallest owl in Africa) and Augur Buzzard may be encountered. The large trees supply food and breeding habitat, while the river seeps below and 'gorras' (deep holes dug by the elephants) provide water to the birds in this arid zone.

www.batisbirdingsafaris.com

Above: Madagascan (Olive) Bee-eater
Right: Namaqua Sandgrouse

Far left: Juvenile Pygmy Falcons
Above left: Adult Pygmy Falcon
Above: Rüppells Korhaan
Left: Damara Red-billed Hornbill

The **Elephants**

Loxondonta Africana

Your first meeting with one of Namibia's desert elephants is a moment you will never forget. Although correctly described as desert 'adapted' elephants they belong to the genus loxodonta africana with the forest elephant of central Africa having the name loxodonta africana cyclotis, and although they are all still classified as a single species many people believe that the forest elephant is of a completely different species.

The desert elephants have adapted to their harsh environment in a number of ways. They are slightly smaller (but still impressive!) to their cousins on the savannah, and have longer legs in proportion to their bodies with larger feet, probably due to the soft sand they frequently encounter. They have adapted so well that they can go without water for up to four days, but from spending time with them I noticed that every other day was their preference. As the waterholes or springs are far apart and the vegetation only follows the riparian riverbeds, they can fill up one evening and then spend the next two days following the course of the ephemeral riverbed at leisure either to their next source of water or returning to the same one.

Left: A very hot day (over 45°C)
Above: Tempers can get frayed!

They also tend to have smaller tusks. Three reasons are mooted for this. In no particular order, it is a known fact that there is a mineral deficiency in their diets that leads to many breakages and cracks so maybe they have just adapted to having smaller tusks. Another is the possibility that they have been subjected to a sort of expedited evolutionary process bought about by the devastating poaching that occurred in the 1980s and 90's, (i.e. the ones with the largest tusks were targeted first), and the other is that maybe they have always been like that, but nobody did any real research on them until peace arrived after independence and the plains of the Masai Mara and the Serengeti would have been a much more inviting proposition to researchers and scientists than the harsh Kaokoland enduring a very messy 20 year bush war.

They tend to be, let's say, less friendly than their savannah counterparts but this again could be because of their memory of the terrible poaching that happened to them in the 70s and 80s and the hunting for food during the war, or it could just be because they rarely see humans and would prefer to keep it that way.

Above: In the Hoanib
Right: Two friends

Apart from that they still keep their same general elephant characteristics often likened to humans but usually only our better ones.

Their main family structure is that the females and young stay in herds and the bulls tend to be either solitary or in pairs, I rarely saw 3 bulls together. The herds (in this area) usually consist of between 8 and 15 elephants made up from newborn calves, through youngsters and teenagers to the younger mothers and aunts (or allomothers) to the matriarch who is usually the oldest (but not always) and most knowledgeable and experienced of the herd.

The matriarch does as you would expect. She decides how long they stay in one place, be it a waterhole or a good area for the food they need at the time, or under a tree for shade during the hottest hours of the day, she decides where and when to go next when they have sated their thirst or the food runs out in the area they are in at the time, drawing from her vast knowledge of hundreds of square kilometres collected over a lifetime of wandering and learning of how the seasonal rains and ephemeral river systems and springs work. She also keeps a careful eye out for danger and will decide whether to flee or fight if anything threatens her charges.

The mothers and aunts (allomothers) take a sort of communal stance looking after the younger ones. A new mother tends to solely look after her newborn and the aunts only step in to help if a baby is threatened or frightened and will quickly gather round to either help or protect any baby in stress. As the calf gets a bit older and begins to become more confidant they will sometimes also step in to help teach it the odd lesson or two but he is usually left to his mother.

Right: Going home

61

Previous pages: Eating bark in the Hoanib
Above: After the 'Let's go' rumble, they all head off to wherever has
been decided.
Far left: Good friends
Middle: Playing with the water
Left: Just because I can!

Once they begin to grow up a bit more, usually after 4 to 5 years the youngsters are usually left much to their own devices unless something serious happens, and they spend their time continuing to learn, usually through play, about how to correlate and associate with their siblings and surroundings. Elephants are born with very few natural instincts (like the apes and dolphins) and nearly everything (apart from getting on their legs as soon as possible after being born, who their mother is, and how to suckle), has to be learnt from their peers. To them, for the first year, their trunk is just some strange thing flapping around in front of their face until they learn to control the 40,000 muscles in six groups that will eventually become their most useful appendage.

Once the calves have grown into teenagers the cows tend to become more responsible and begin to help more with the general wellbeing of the herd until eventually they become mothers themselves. The bulls are a different matter though. As they get older they start sparing and play-fighting with their peers. This gradually gets more and more disruptive as their testosterone levels rise until eventually they are pushed out of the herd to begin their adult life.

They will then spend a few years wandering their region, learning to avoid the older stronger bulls and gradually making their own home range (not territory) which can consist of hundreds of square kilometres, occasionally coming into conflict with humans on the way and often breaking through the fences to Etosha or the veterinary fence while following the routes passed on to them through countless generations. Then occasionally seeking out a herd when in musth, but usually being quickly ousted by any dominant bulls present, until they have grown in stature and have enough experience to eventually find their own herd to begin the cycle all over again.

Right: Even though Elephants seem cumbersome they can often be quite agile. If they want to go somewhere, they will…

Elephants have amazingly complex forms of communication that we still do not understand and maybe never will completely, despite all the research that is ongoing.

There are many of the obvious ones that we all know and the trunk has several of them. These range from a mock charge with the trunk out and ears flapping, usually with a loud trumpet to the trunk tucked in and ears back for serious business. They raise it in the air away from the ground, to get 'clean air' to scent if they suspect that there may be a threat nearby, if they are interested in something or maybe a bull in musth seeking a cow in oestrous. Calves can sometimes be seen sucking their trunks as a sort or reassurance. Quite often one elephant will put it's trunk in another's mouth as a sort of bonding between either current friends or one not seen for a while. The youngsters are often seen entwining their trunks as a playful gesture between fellow elephants, usually of a similar age.

The more complex forms of communication though are the sounds they produce. The easy one we all know is the trumpet, which is used either when something (or you) surprises an elephant (not advised...) or when he/she wants to wants to warn something or somebody that they are not welcome. The young males tend to practice this quite a lot but with the older ones it's best to take notice.

The more difficult communication sounds are the rumbles of which humans can hear only a fraction.

Right: An evening dust bath

The Dung Beetle.

(Scarabaeoidea)

Throughout the world it is estimated that there are over 5000 different species of dung beetles, with Antarctica being the only continent lacking them, for obvious reasons.

They play a very important roll in the ecology of the region. Firstly they are attracted to the dung by scent, when they reach their target they bury themselves in the dung and start their work. After a short while the surface will break open and they will emerge with a perfectly formed ball that can be up to 40 times their own weight, they then proceed to roll the ball in a completely straight line, despite various obstacles in the way, occasionally having to fight off other beetles trying to steal their prize. More often than not there is both a male and female sharing the work although sometimes the female is just catching a free ride. Nobody is too sure what makes them so insistent on following such a straight line to wherever they have chosen to go to, I noticed that the wind sometimes had an influence (they would tend to go downwind, presumably going back in the direction to where they first 'smelt' the dung), but the Scarabaeus zambesianus has been shown to use polarized light from moonlight.

When they finally reach their destination they bury their ball and mate underground. The female will then lay her egg or eggs inside the ball in a form of mass provisioning.

In this manner, dung beetles play a very important roll in keeping the African landscape a lot tidier than it would be otherwise (also helping to keep fly populations down), and are very valuable in helping to return important nutrients to the soils.

It is thought that they have a sort of 'language' (for want of a better word) using these rumbles, that will probably never be fully understood as it is so alien to our ideas of communication. Once, watching about 40 elephants, scattered all over the plains at Hobatere, grazing on the lush new grass after the rains and generally not doing much else, I decided to clean a lens and took my eyes of them for about 5 minutes. When I looked up again, they all had gathered together. They stayed in a group for another few minutes with the odd youngster not paying much attention and then all moved off together, as if one, towards the west. I heard no rumbles nor saw any particular physical signs of what was going on and can only put this down to some other form of communication. Obviously this was all to do with their infrasound that they use and we cannot hear, but personally I would be reticent to liken them to humans having a 'chat' about where to go. To me, that is an easy way to try to simplify and to humanise something we cannot and may never understand.

Research has also shown that they can use this infrasound to communicate over large distances, possibly picking up the signals through the pads of their feet. This sounds very likely, especially when when you see various herds appear at the same place on the same day (after many months apart) from all different points of the compass.

Elephants are herbivores, being both browsers and grazers, depending on what is available at the time and what their bodies need.

Left: Note the broken tusks, due to a mineral deficiency in their diet.
Above: A calf interested in the poisonous euphobia.

They will eat most plants but obviously in this area the greener the better as there is more moisture in the vegetation. When there is new lush grass after the rains, they gather it up in their trunks in huge sheaths and continuously supply their mouths like a conveyer belt, until they can't eat any more. Acacia trees (camelthorn) also are a favourite, thorns and all. After the seeds have formed they can often be found shaking the trees to make the seedpods fall and then delicately picking them up individually with their trunks one by one. Of course not all are picked up, much to the delight of the local giraffe and oryx as they have high concentrations of protein. They also like eating bark. In this area they seem to prefer it off fallen as opposed to living trees and so tend not as destructive as elephants on other parts of the continent.

Why they sometimes chew on anthills I have no idea. Maybe something to do with minerals.

The elephants have a long life, usually 60 to 70 years, and throughout this, they have a supply of new teeth to replace the ones worn down by their coarse diet. Elephants usually have 6 pairs of molars throughout their life, growing in size for each set of which only 2 pairs are used at any one time. When worn out they are replaced by new ones growing from behind. The sixth molars weigh from 4 to 5 kilograms and have a grinding length of up to 25cm. Very rarely a seventh set is produced but these tend to be small.

This continues until they are about 65-70 years old when the last set is finally worn away.

After this, the elephant will return to the earth, dying either of malnutrition or starvation.

The 'desert adapted' elephants are generally less destructive than their cousins living in areas with more food available. Although the above images would suggest otherwise, fifteen minutes later there was not a single leaf left on the fallen branch, whereas in other, more lush parts of Africa they might just take a few mouthfuls and then move on to the next tree.

The **Himba**

Above: Chief Thongora Maundjua from near Swartbooisdrift.
Left: A very remote village (as yet there are still no vehicle tracks to be seen).

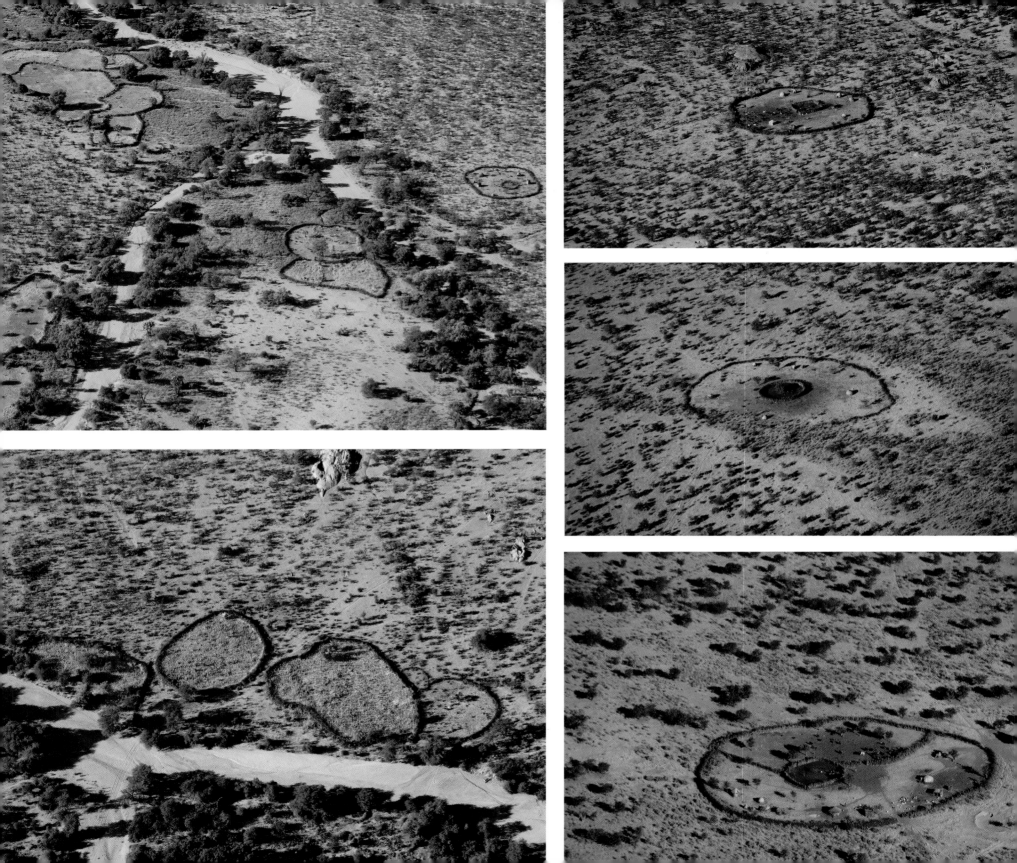

The Himba are semi-nomadic pastoralists who mainly inhabit the Kaokoland part of the region but also live in the southern part of Angola. Unlike many other indigenous groups in Africa, they have managed to maintain some of their traditional lifestyle, owing mainly to the fact that the land they occupy is so harsh and unyielding that in the past it has been rarely coveted by the colonialists and commercial farmers that have affected so many other regions of the continent. New hydro-electricity proposals, mining and the advance of tourism may take their toll though.

The Himba moved into present-day Namibia as part of a larger migration of Bantu-speaking peoples from east Africa several hundred years ago. About 200 years ago, the group began to split and a large group known as the Herero moved southward, while the ancestors of the present-day Himba remained.

Left: Different shapes of their living enclosures and those to protect their crops

Today, the Himba still generally try to live as they have for centuries and manage to eke out an existence by following their herds of goats and cattle to new grazing areas and waterholes as existing areas become exhausted. They live in small settlements or family groups throughout Kaokoland, sometimes living in the same village for years if the annual rains are plentiful. If not they will move to another area and return when there is enough grazing for their livestock.

The homes of the Himba are simple, cone-shaped structures of saplings, bound together with palm leaves and plastered with mud and dung.

The characteristic look of the Himba comes from intricate hairstyles, traditional clothing, the use of personal adornments, as well as the use of a mixture of red ochre, butter and resin from the Omuzumba shrub.

This paste is known as ëotjizeí is used as protection against the sun and as a skin lotion. It is rubbed on the skin, into hair and onto traditional clothing. In towns they tend to wear western clothing, although in Opuwo (the administrative centre of the area) many traditional Himbas are seen going about their daily life, in the more inaccessible areas of Kaokoland where towns and settlements with western influences are few and far between it is very much the norm.

Above: Young boys practicing their dance routine.
Right: Competition for the milk!

81

Most Himba children now attend school. Radio brings news, music and entertainment from further a field. Also faced with a life of hardship, particularly in times of drought and hunger, many young Himba men choose to work in towns and villages. This can bring on the usual problems with alcohol and the law.

But development also brings challenges, threats and controversy. A proposed mega-dam on the Kunene river would bring hydro electricity to Namibia, but it would also flood many square miles of traditional homelands and ancestral gravesites and also bring in thousands of foreign workers that with their roads and necessary ancillary infrastructure, would permanently transform the region. The Himbas in southern Angola though, seem to have been left more to their own devices.

The Himba's day starts early. Women arise before or at dawn and apply otjize. Before the cattle are herded to the grazing areas, they are milked by the women, often on one side only leaving the other side free for the calves. Each homestead has two fires, a small one inside the hut for warmth and a larger one outside, for cooking. Once the cattle are milked, the men herd them to the grazing area. If the grazing is poor, the entire village will move to a place where there is better grazing. Young men often set up separate, temporary villages and move around with the cattle, leaving the women, children and older men at the main homestead.

Left: They remove one or two of the women's front teeth at an early age, as this is though of as a sign of beauty
Right: Multitasking

Once married, the women leave their villages and move to the villages of their husbands where they adopt their rules. Himba men are not monogamous and may have a number of wives and children in different homesteads. Women are not monogamous either and may have a number of partners. However courtship and relationships are bound by strict rules and modes of behavior.

After a woman has given birth, mother and child spend a some time at a special shelter built to the side of the headman's hut, near the sacred fire, under special protection of the ancestral spirits. After this time has passed (about a week in our way of thinking how time passes), the child is brought to the sacred fire and introduced to the spirits of the ancestors by the headman. The child is given names from the patrilineal and matrilineal lines, ensuring that the origins of the child are known. The child remains with its mother until about the age of three, after which it lives with its siblings.

Although Himba children are very independent, they are cared for by all the members of the family in the homestead. Between the ages of 10 and 12, the bottom two or four incisor teeth of the child are knocked out in a ceremony that is believed to protect the child from dangerous influences and ensure the protection of the ancestors.

Young males are circumcised and have a coming of age rituals. Young girls also have a coming of age ceremony.

Women tend to spend the day close to the settlement. They occupy themselves with cooking, gardening, milking cattle, looking after children, caring for livestock in the kraal and making clothes, jewellery and the traditional ochre and butter paste, otjize.

Flour is made from maize and butter is churned. Wood has to be collected, and water has to be carried from wells. The children help with the tasks.

The diet of the Himba consists mainly of a porridge made from maize and milk.

Milk left over after making the porridge is used to make butter, which is churned in gourds hanging from a branch in a small tree.

Although meat is occasionally part of the Himba diet, beef is consumed sparingly as cattle represent the wealth of a clan. Meat from small stock such as goats and chickens is more likely to be found in the Himba diet.

When cattle are slaughtered, it is usually done at a ceremony.

The Himba homestead is a family unit, overseen by the headman who is normally a grandfather and the oldest male in the village. Most social systems either follow the lineage of the father (the patrilineal aspect), or the mother (the matrilineal aspect).

The Himba social system uses both and a Himba person belongs to both sides. The headman is responsible for residence, religious aspects of life embodied by the sacred fire and ensuring that the rules of tradition and the specific rules of the clan are obeyed.

The matrilineal aspect is responsible for movable property and economic matters such as handling of money and property. The Himba headman is the ultimate authority is identified by an erenge bracelet.

The sacred fire represents the ancestors of the Himbas, and is kept burning 24 hours a day. The Himba believe in a god who created everything (Mukuru), but this god is very remote, and communication only takes place through the spirits of male ancestors. The male leader, the headman, of the Himba clan sits by the fire during the day and talks to the ancestors about problems facing the family.

He oversees births, marriages and coming of age ceremonies. He performs the various ceremonies at the sacred fire, involving the spirits of the ancestors in the daily life of the village. He is also responsible for the rules of the tribe.

If a crime is committed or a property dispute arises, he will be called to give judgment. If his judgment is not accepted, a number of headmen will meet to discuss the matter.

When a Himba dies, the body is wrapped and bound in the skin of cattle and placed next to the sacred fire. The first period of mourning lasts 24 hours or more, during which time cattle are slaughtered.

The person is buried far from the village, and the horns of the slaughtered cattle are placed on the grave. The greater the number of horns on the grave, the greater the wealth and status of the individual.

In the case of a headman, the main hut is dismantled and parts of it are burned. The sacred fire is scattered, to be rekindled later from

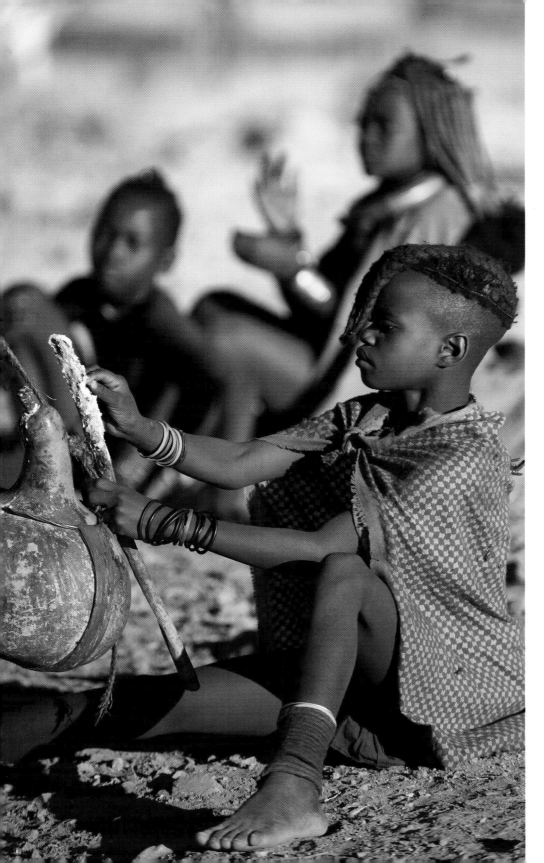

new Mopane branches. The headman is bound wrapped in the skin of his favorite ox and buried facing the rising sun in the east. His walking stick is broken in two and placed on the grave along with his sandals and the horn that he used for calling cattle. The elder is believed to enter the afterlife accompanied by the cattle that are slaughtered during the mourning period. After the person is buried, the clan returns to the homestead and a second period of mourning begins, lasting about a month.

More cattle are slaughtered and their horns will be added to those already on the grave. The ancestors are contacted by burning the root of the Omuhe shrub, and a purification ritual takes place. Cattle owned by deceased males will often be inherited by the family of the deceased male's sister, normally the male son. In the case of the death of a woman, the homestead will be inherited by a brother, or if the woman has no surviving brother, by the eldest child of a sister. In this way cattle rights and property rights are continuously redistributed through families.

The Himbas are a proud race and have learned to live in one of the harshest environments on our planet and although some are adopting western clothing and our way of life there are many to be found off the beaten track that adhere strongly to their traditional way of life.

Left: Churning the milk in a gourd to make butter

The **Skeleton Coast**

Beautiful Desolation

Although strictly not part of Kaokoland and Damaraland this National Park demands a mention and is well worth visiting if you have time.

The region is a long, desolate, thin strip of land that runs for 600km (16,000sqKm) from the Ugab river in the south to the Kunene river in the north. It's climate and consequent wildlife is governed by the freezing upwelling of the Benguella current that sweeps up the Namibian coastline all the way from Antarctica. The region rarely receives more than 10mm (0.39in) of rainfall in any one year but on many days, huge fogbanks roll in from the Atlantic to bring in much needed moisture. This fog, combined with the detrius blown in by the east winds from inland, supports a huge variety of life including beetles, lizards, snakes and some birds. It is *very* much a living desert. This fog also sometimes reaches into Damaraland and Kaokoland helping out the smaller animals in their quest for water and likewise the rivers can also sometimes reach the sea, giving the larger animals an extended browsing corridor down to the coast.

Right: The Kunene River reaches the ocean

The Skeleton coast is dominated by vast dune fields (or the sand-sea), gravel plains or salt flats. The actual shore line itself, is constantly pounded by surf and is mainly soft, (i.e. sandy) interspersed with rocky outcrops that make excellent breeding grounds for the many cape fur seals that take full advantage of the ocean's prolific sea life, produced by the combination of a nutrient rich upwelling and ample African sunlight that starts off the food-chain. Opportunistic brown hyena, black-backed jackals and occasionally lions are sometimes seen scouring the beach, in their search for an unwary seal pup or two, but a lack of fresh water makes this an extremely rare occurrence.

Bird life is prolific with huge flocks of terns and cormorants travelling to and from their feeding, nesting and roosting grounds, to flamingos taking advantage of the algae and brine shrimps to be found in the salt flats.

Above: Cape Fur Seals have numerous colonies along the coast
Next page: Water seepage finally meets the South Atlantic

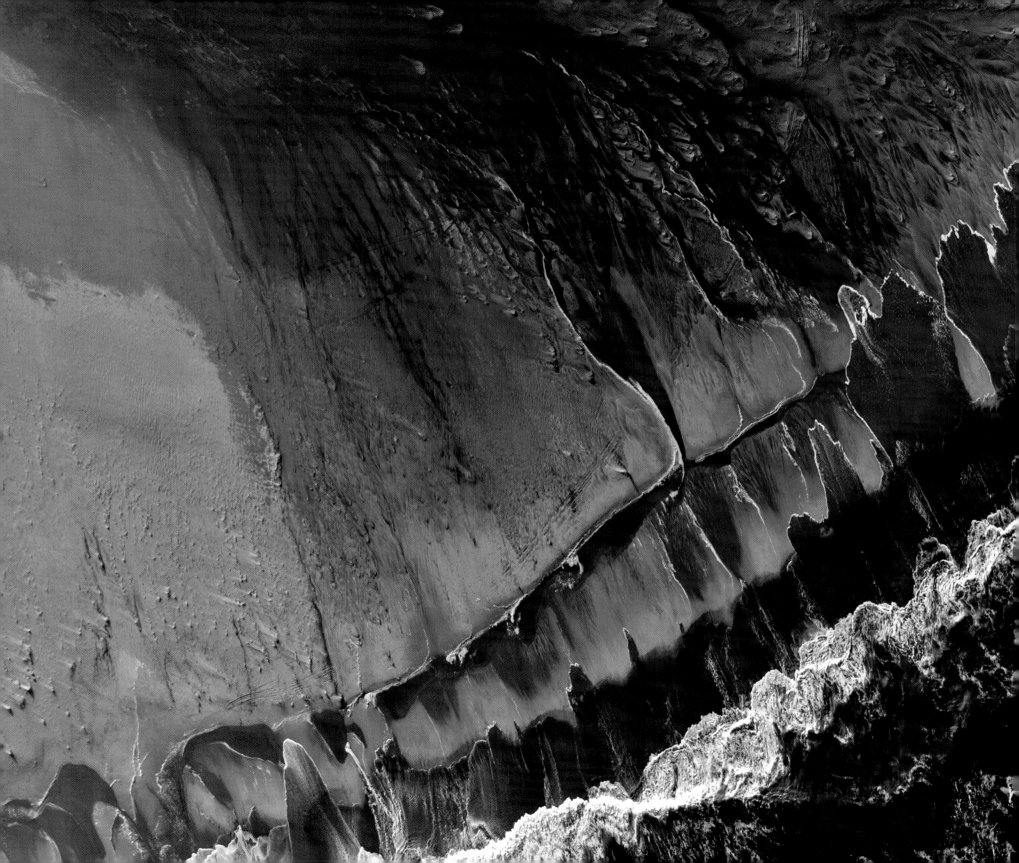

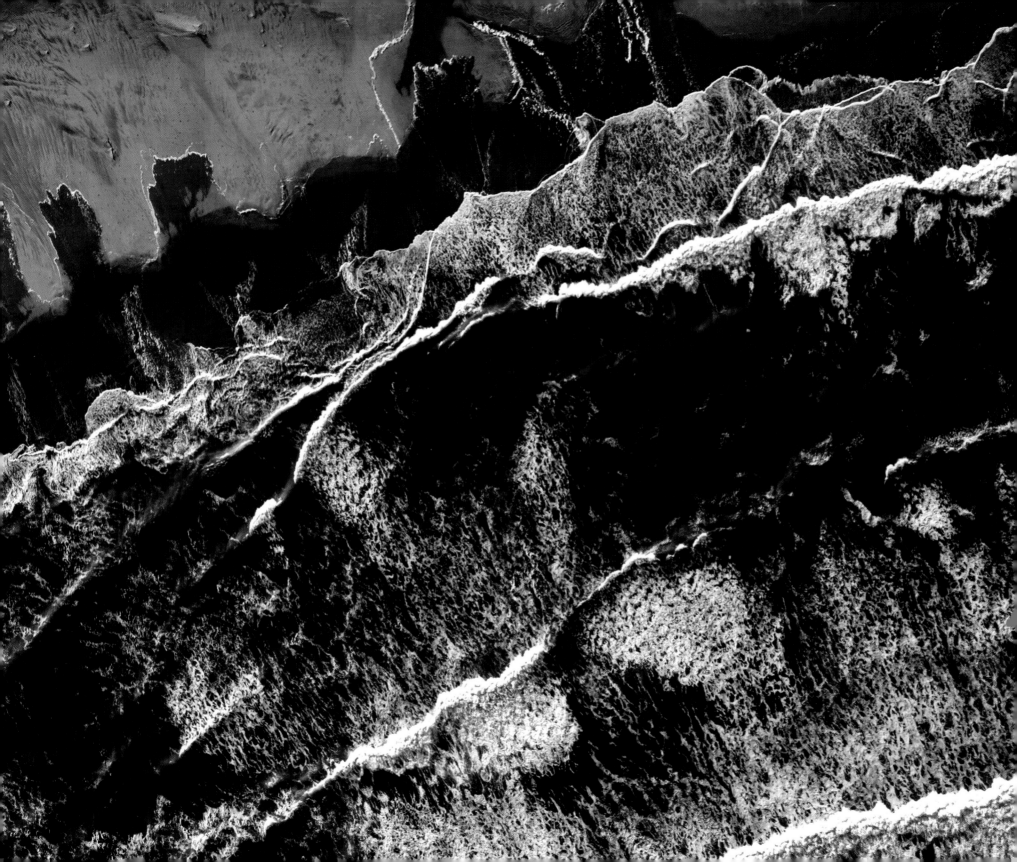

Above: Barchan dunes form majestic shapes
Far right: The 'Clay Castles' of the Hourasib

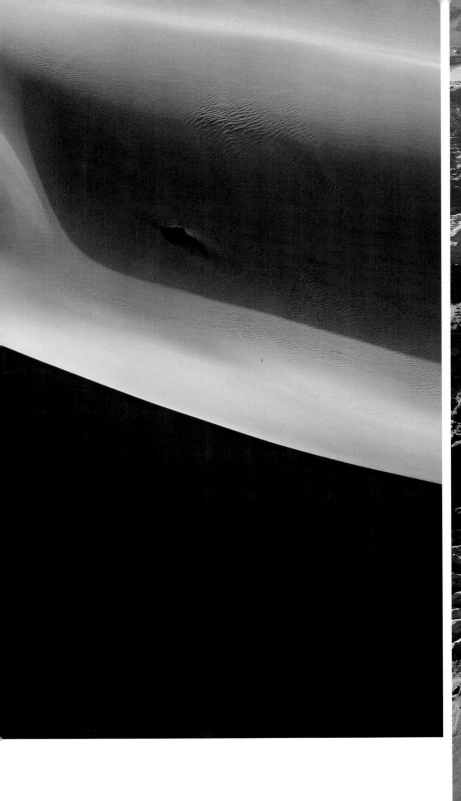

Above: Cormorants prefer islands like these as they afford protection against predators
Right: Salt pans. The colours come from the algae that live in the saline waters

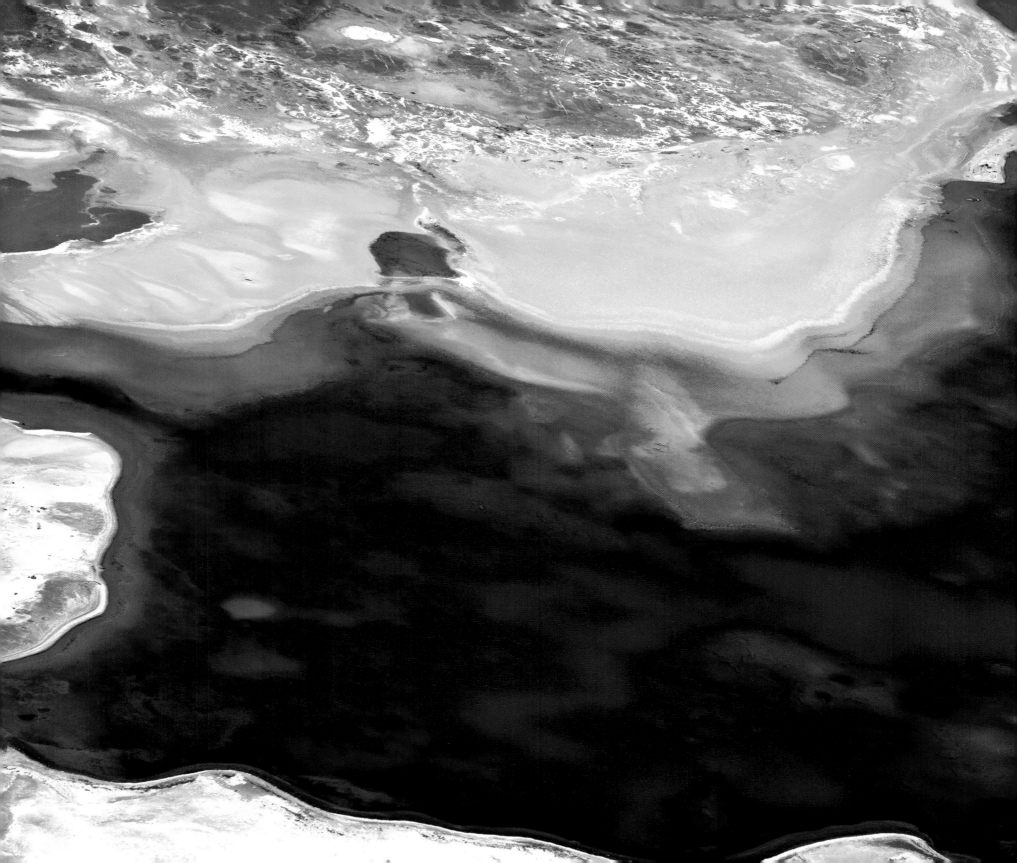

One of the prime sources of food for jackals and brown hyena is the constant source of dead seals washed up

Cape Fur Seal nursing her pup

Cormorants sunning themselves before another fishing trip in the freezing ocean

Flamingos in the evening light

Behind the Camera

Transport and accommodation

I needed a vehicle to see me through the rough terrain of the Kunene region and also to be my home and office for what ended up to be the next 20 months and 35,000km.

Obviously I had to have a 4x4 and it had to be tough enough to take anything that Kaokoland could throw at it, from crossing rivers (I tended to avoid those though as I was often on my own, and being stuck in a flowing river with nobody to help didn't seem like a very good idea) to tracking rhinos across rocky landscapes and deep sand.

Luckily I managed to find a little used, one year old, Land Rover 110 2.5 TDi (one lady owner!) who ended up looking after me perfectly. Not only did she start every time, first time but she gave me excellent ground clearance and a nice high vantage point from either inside, or on the roof.

After the formalities with police roadworthy checks and registration were over, various adaptations and additions were needed to be sorted .

Top: Driving at night has its dangers
Middle: The 'Poort' in the Hourasib where there was usually a large bull elephant waiting to ambush me on the other side!
Bottom: Heading off at dawn

The rugged terrain that the Land Rover took in its stride

The Land Rover already had a roof-rack, ladder, duel battery system, and a long range fuel tank fitted, but these were not enough. Additional items to be fitted and added were an integrated water tank, spare wheel carrier on the rear door, various 12v electrical outlets, a 1200W inverter, holders for an extra 60 liters fuel in jerrycans on the roof, a roof-tent (rarely used), 75w solar panel and regulator, 60 ltr fridge/freezer, sump guard, extra spare wheels and tires, an awning and a multitude of other items from fire extinguishers and first aid boxes to camping and cooking equipment.

I was used to sailing yachts across the Atlantic and living at 6,000ft in the Italian Alps but this was all new to me.

By the time I had finished, it had become quite difficult to accommodate any passengers, especially as the front passenger area was usually used to hold all the camera equipment for easy access and a third of the rear seat had been removed to house the fridge/freezer (so that I could access it from the front), the remainder taken up by various items that would not fit elsewhere.

On a couple of occasions I did try to accommodate a fellow traveller /photographer but it didn't really work, as usually, to photograph the subject, whether it be elephants or smaller you have to position your vehicle so you can get the best shot from your vantage point/window, as often it is not advisable to get out of your car. Not only because of any danger you might put yourself into, but mainly because the animals do not normally see a vehicle as a threat unless it gets too close (although both black rhinos and elephants sometimes haven't read the rule book), but they do see a human form as a very real threat. Consequently only one of the vehicle's occupants was in a position to be able to get a good view. After a few attempts any passengers were put on the roof. The only change that I might make next time would be to look at the 130 instead of the 110.

Above: The Khowarib Schlucht

The roof tent was rarely used, as I was usually up before dawn to catch the light and back after dark and putting it up and down in the dark was not that tempting. What was used most was the ground tent. This was convenient as I could make a proper camp for a few days and go out tracking the animals early morning and again in the late afternoon returning to light a fire before darkness fell.

One thing to always remember was to keep the tent door closed so that no uninvited guests could also make it their new home and give me a nasty surprise in the night. Near Rhino camp I did wake up one morning to find rather large paw prints around the tent from the night before, and occasionally elephants would pass by, or jackals would check out the camp, but otherwise I was generally left alone. Whenever possible though, I would prefer to sleep under the stars.

During this period, Hobatere was my main base in the region and Steve and Louise Braine, and family very kindly let me store unneeded equipment there whilst I was in the bush. They also fed and watered me generously and shared much of their vast knowledge of the region.

Hermann and Emile at Palmwag Lodge were also very helpful along with Piete and Rudy from Save the Rhino Trust.

Far up in the north of the region, on the border with Angola, Pete and Hilary Morgan at Kunene River Lodge were always a pleasure to spend a few days with and wash some of the dust off, when not annoying crocodiles in the river or trying to sneak up on their cinderella waxbills.

Last but not least for the aerial photography, Matthias Braune of Bataleur Aviation based in Swakopmund was a huge help and we spent many thrilling hours hanging out of various Cessnas where a door should have been, photographing the vast, beautiful expanses of dunes, rivers and mountains.

Top: My other form of transport
Middle: A camp at 'Leopard Rock'
Bottom: A camp at the Hoanib River

Cameras

The cameras used for this book were mainly digital Nikon with Nikkor lenses. There is no 'ideal' camera system, they all have their pros and cons. The reason I use Nikon is that I have used it for 25 years now and have had no major breakdowns, the cameras were used in a harsh environment for 18 months and I had no issues with dust on the sensors and the lenses , focussing speed and vibration control are exceptional. Last but not least I could use the cameras instinctively without having to look at the controls to see what I was doing.

Nearly every picture in this book was taken 'hand held' with no tripod although a bean bag, the odd branch of a tree and the car window wound down to the right height were useful when using the 200-400mm or 300mm for a long period waiting for something to happen!

Not many 'gadgets' were used, but I found a tripod and a radio remote control useful when I needed to be aware of the whole surroundings and not just what I could see through the viewfinder (ie. a weaver bird returning to it's nest).

I mainly used 3 cameras, 2 D700s, one with a 200-400mm f4 lens, the other with a 70-200mm f2.8, and a D300 with a 105mm Macro. The main reasons for using the 2 D700s with their dedicated lenses was that I could quickly swap cameras as the situation changed, by not having to constantly change lenses I reduced the possibility of getting dust into the cameras considerably and finally if one broke for any reason I still had another. These two lenses were used for about 90% of the images with the remaining 10% made up from a 24-70mm f2.8, 60mm f2.8macro, 105mm f2.8 macro. I had a tele-converter but never used it as I found in tests that it degraded the image too much and the quality of the sensors in the D700s was so good that it was better to crop later if needed.

For the panoramic images I found it better to take a series of shots and then to 'photomerge' them in Photoshop later. All the lenses had either skylight or UV filters attached for protection, no 'effects' filters were used apart from a circular polarizing filter for the occasional landscape to help bring out the clouds as I prefer to show my images 'as seen' rather than enhanced by various gadgets and accessories and computer enhancement.

A canon G9 was useful in towns to help avoid unwanted attention, and to look more like a tourist but still gave me decent quality RAW files.

Computers and communications

My main computer was a Mac Book Pro, with a 2.53GHz processor, 4GB memory and 320GB hard drive, in addition to this I took along an old Power Book G4 as backup which thankfully was never needed. Out of preference I would have used film, but this was not feasible due to all the reasons you already know. Times change...

Four Lacie 'Rugged' external hard drives were also taken. Two were kept with me and the other two were left at a couple of lodges in the region and were updated whenever I passed by, consequently if a disaster happened I could lose a maximum of 2-3 weeks work, luckily they were not needed. To power all this and to keep the cameras going I had a duel battery system in the Land Rover with a battery monitor, one for the engine and another for the 'domestic' supply. Both of these were charged by the alternator when the engine was running.

To save on fuel, noise, disturbance etc I had a 75watt solar panel installed. When deployed it had a 15m lead which meant that the car could be in the shade under a tree whilst the panel could be in the sun. Between 10:00 and 14:00 I found I could run the computer, re-charge camera batteries and keep the fridge/freezer running on full as well as keeping the battery topped up ready for evening and night-time use. The panel gave me useful electricity from about 2 hours either side of sunrise and sunset as long as it was pointed directly at the sun itself, which was useful because between 10:00 and 16:00 the sun was too harsh to photograph most things anyway. I also had two AA battery chargers that were used for torch batteries lanterns etc. A LED head-torch has now been oficially upgraded from 'gadget' to a necessity.

Communications were a bit of a problem, but not insurmountable but at a cost. Obviously 'roaming' on my UK mobile phone was out of the question due to cost so a local SIM card was bought fairly quickly, this was fine for local and international texts and local calls. The next problem was sending and receiving e-mails and so a 'dangle' had to be bought for the computer, but these rely on cellphone coverage and where I was working that was very intermittent. There were three ways of getting connected when I was near any sort of civilization. The first was to use the 'dongle' and trust MTC's connection and pay for a very slow connection by the minute, the second was to go to a lodge's reception area and buy a card with a password for x amount of minutes, this is faster but more expensive, so you have to be quick, and if there was a lot to be done the third was to stay in an expensive place that had free internet access!

Finally because of the remoteness of where I was working, and usually alone without anybody knowing my route for up to three weeks at a time,I decided that a satellite telephone would be a sensible idea. Luckily (again) this was never used in anger...

Glossary of animals

English name	Afrikaans name	Scientific name
Mammals		
African Elephant	Olifant	Loxodonta africana
Bat Eared Fox	Bakoorjakkals	Otocyon megalotis
Black-backed Jackal	Rooijakkals	Canis mesomelas
Black Rhino	Leeu	Diceros bicornis
Cape Fur Seal	Kaapse pelsrob	Arctocephalus pusillus
Cheetah	Jagluiperd	Acinonyx jubatus
Genet (Lesser spotted)	Kleinkolmuskejaatkat	Genetta genetta
Giraffe	Kameelperd	Giraffa camelopardis
Hartmann's Mountain Zebra	Hartmann se bergkwagga	Equs zebra hartmannae
Klipspringer	Klipspringer	Oreotragus oerotragus
Leopard	Luiperd	Panthera pardus
Lion	Leeu	Panthera leo
Meerkat	Stokstertmeerkat	Suricata suricatta
Oryx	Gemsbok	Oryx gazella
Spotted Hyena	Gevekte Hiëna	Crocuta crocuta
Warthog	Vladvark	Phacochoerus aethopicus
Birds		
Hammercop	Hammercop	Scopus umbretta
Pearl-spotted Owlet	Witkoluil	Glaucidium perlatum
Augur Buzzard	Witborsjakkalsvoël	Buteo rufofuscus
African Pygmy Falcon	Dwergvalk	Polihierax semitorquatus
Rüppell's Korhaan	Woestynkorhaan	Eupodotis rueppellii
Madagascar Olive Bee-eater	Olyfbyvreter	Merops superciliosus
Damara Red-billed Hornbill	Damararooibekneushoringvoël	Tockus damarensis
Namaqua Sandgrouse	Kelkiewyn	Pterosles namaqua

Acknowledgements

Throughout my travels in Namibia, there was never a dull moment. Every morning I would wake up just before dawn and think "Now I wonder what is going to happen today"? Usually there was some sort of adventure just around the corner! So after 2 years in such a remote area, and nothing disastrous had happened, I thought it time to get back to civilisation and put this book together. I had got away with not being trampled by elephants, or eaten by lions, no snakes had bitten me or scorpions stung me, and I'd not contracted any tropical disease!

Although I spent much time in remote areas I still had to get back to civilisation occasionally, usually to get a service done on the Land Rover or to buy a new set of tyres.

At the beginning Martin from Ultimate safaris helped by selling me such a reliable Land Rover (½ a litre of oil in 35,000km), and helped with the endless paperwork for work permits and visas. They also arrange safaris to this region.

Matthias Braune from Bataleur Aviation in Swakopmund was an incredible help with the aerial photography. Without him none of the stunning aerial views would have been possible.

One person who helped me enormously in the beginning was Charles Norwood from Safari Drive, whose knowledge of Southern Africa was immensely useful about Land Rovers and African driving. His Land Rovers are all in excellent condition and fully equipped for this kind of adventure.

Vincent Bruna from Passion Safari was always a pleasure to cross paths with, whether in Damaraland, Kaokoland, Walvis Bay or Windhoek. His wealth of knowledge about the area is immense and he was always a pleasure to travel with occasionally.

Also without the help of the Braine family at Hobatere this book would never been possible. Unfortunately after many years there, they have now moved on and are concentrating on their new birding company as a family concern, specialising in Namibia and Angola, but also other countries if desired. Their knowledge and love of our feathered friends (and most other things) is quite extraordinary.

In addition, there were many other helpful people, from Hilary and Pete at Kunene River Lodge, to Derek at Etendecka Lodge, and Herman and Emile at Palmwag. Vayna at Land Rover in Walvis Bay service department, Michael at Erongo Auto Electric, Kevin at Radio Electronic in Walvis Bay, Liz and Cees at the Spindrift Lodge, and Helene and family at The Lagoon Lodge, again both in Walvis Bay.

Finally to all the people who helped from the Save The Rhino Trust, in particular Piete Beytell, who is now with the Ministry of Environment and Tourism (MET) looking after the rhinos countrywide.

Some pages to add your own memories